PA

Sharing

by Shelly Nielsen
illustrated by
Virginia Kylberg

Published by Abdo & Daughters, 6535 Cecilia Circle, Edina, Minnesota 55439

Edited by: Rosemary Wallner

Library of Congress Cataloging-in-Publication Data

Nielsen, Shelly, 1958-
     Sharing / written by Shelly Nielsen ; edited by Rosemary Wallner.
        p. cm. -- (Values matter)
     Summary: Poems portray sharing--of things and time and self.
     ISBN 1-56239-063-5
     1. Sharing -- Juvenile poetry. 2. Children's poetry, American.
[1. Sharing -- Poetry. 2. Conduct of life – Poetry. 3. American poetry.]
I. Wallner, Rosemary, 1964-   . II. Title. III. Series: Nielsen, Shelly, 1958-
Values matter.
PS3564.I354S52 1992   811'.54--dc20   91-73045
                                            CIP
                                          AC

Sharing

Abdo & Daughters
Minneapolis

Time Share

Aunt Lois asked me to come and bake
her recipe for lemon cake.
I was watching my favorite show,
but I got right up and put on my coat.
Even though I love cartoons,
I'd rather share Aunt Lois' afternoon.

Stories to Share

A sister is a pesky critter,
I'd rather play
than baby-sit her.
Sarah tap dances
and blows messy soap bubbles…
Sisters are a peck of trouble!
But one thing we both like to do
is read a book all the way through.
I say the words;
she turns the pages.
We sisters share stories for ages and ages.

My Toys

Hands off!
Those toys are mine!
Don't ruin my blocks,
Don't touch my train.
And stay away from my bicycle, too.
I am not going to share with you.
Don't fly my kite,
Don't use my paints,
And, no, you may not play my game.
No matter what you may say,
I am not sharing today.
But...
it's lonely playing all alone.
I changed my mind.
I'll share, Tyrone.

Zap!

I love to make the TV switch…
just hit a button and *zap*!
But then my crabby brother yells,
"Hey, I was watching that!"
Now we take turns choosing shows:
first Dennis picks, then me.
To get along with a brother,
it helps to share the TV.

Choices, Choices

I have to choose.
What will it be--
     a present for Dean
     or something for me?
Although I'd like
to buy this toy--
sharing with Dean
will bring *both* of us joy.

Our Room

Welcome to the room I share
with my little brother.
My bed is on this side of things,
and Trent's is on the other.
He kindly shares his window with me,
and I share the closet door;
and sometimes very late at night,
we share a spooky story.

Cold Weather Friend

When it's cold and blowy
and your lips are turning blue,
it's good to have a friend with pockets
who will share her mittens with you.

Sleepover

Yay! Yahoo! Grandma's here!
She's come to stay for a week.
And while she's staying at my house
she'll need a place to sleep.
I know where Grandma can snooze:
in my cozy bed.
She can snuggle under
my teddy bear sheets,
with my pillow under her head.

Have a Seat

On the bus when it's crowded,
I let others have my seat.
It feels grown-up
to hold on tight
and sway on my feet.

Lemon Drops

Yum, yum
lemon drops.
How many in a bag?
Five for me,
and five for Scott,
and one to share with the dog.
Lemon drops taste delicious
melting on your tongue;
but they taste even better
when there's some for everyone!

Plenty of Pennies!

Piles of pennies,
mountains high.
Hundreds and thousands,
stacked to the sky.
I've saved and saved...
what will my pennies buy?
Food for children,
so they don't cry.

I Shared It!

Found a nickel--
    shared it!
Pink Popsicle--
    shared it!
Had a pickle--
    shared it!
Got a tickle--
    shared it!

Flowers For You

Pick some pansies for your teacher,
a pretty handful
for her to keep--
  yellows,
    purples,
      pinks,
        and whites--
and watch her face light up bright.

What's So Funny?

My favorite thing to share
is a joke with a friend;
we laugh until our stomachs ache
and then tell the joke again.